Bobcat Country

Also by Brandi Homan

Hard Reds (2008)

Bobcat Country

Brandi Homan

Shearsman Books
Exeter

First published in the United Kingdom in 2010 by
Shearsman Books Ltd
58 Velwell Road
Exeter EX4 4LD

www.shearsman.com

ISBN 978-1-84861-085-9
First Edition

Acknowledgements

See page 79.

For Bex and H and Bobcats Everywhere

Let us all be from somewhere.
Let us tell each other everything we can.
—Bob Hicok

TABLE OF CONTENTS

DOWN HOME

RECURRING DREAM HOUSE

DRUGSTORE COWGIRL

MOBILE HOMECOMING

DOWN HOME

The vacillating demands of mediocrity must be satisfied
—Aleksandar Hemon

WHAT IT MEANS TO BE AN AMERICAN

It's a picnic. Buckets of beer, a bluegrass band, a shotgun
wedding. Casseroles in covered dishes, sparklers, fireflies.
Doritos and French fries. Canteloupe squares and a waitress
humming in the background.

On pontoon boats, we want to waterski. We're all on ecstasy,
sour cream for a smooth tongue. Everything slides into the lake.
Our lifejackets are swollen, our cells blowin' up.
Our Mastercards work. Our teeth sparkle.

A Simpson sister tries to sing. Half of us are pregnant.
The other half are sterile. This is not a dystopia, so obviously
dystopic—our knives keep getting bigger.
None of us can stop eating.

COUPLES SKATE

Everybody deserves a balloon, a big one tied to a car on a
sale lot. Someone is always crying *Daddy, Daddy*, but I look
good on paper—put the tips of my thumbs together and
relax your eyes. A two-nailed mini-thumb will appear.

I love eating crow all the time, am SO done with kissing
people I don't want to. It's past the point where I'm allowed
to go without makeup. The waiter is cute, though, and
gentle with my earrings. He orders a Glenlivet and jokes
about playing the baby grand.

Smoochy, smoochy, we make out to Dokken. I'm a smitten
kitten all right, woo boy.

Guitar solo!

He tells me to tone it down but I cry until my nose bleeds.
I have some screaming left. Really I just want to look pretty
because you know, snow blows horizontally here and I'm
tired of *The problem with my girlfriend is . . .*

He leads me back into the rink. I crossover on command,
have forgotten how to toe-stop. Nice girls know to skate
backwards.

GOOD CHINA

My ex-future-mother-in-law used to be a cop, but when she retired she started selling antiques on eBay. Soon, there was a whole "inventory" in her basement, with stainless steel shelves and everything. She'd show us her loot after estate sales.

Once I noticed she had a set of china like my mother's. The good china, the kind we only brought out for holidays or if we were expecting the President or something. It was white with little blue flowers and had silver around the edges.

My ex-future-mother-in-law pointed to the china and said how beautiful it was, her favorite of the china she'd seen. I smiled and told her my mother had the same set, that she had bought it piece by piece at the grocery store as a part of an ongoing promotion.

Well, she said, it's my favorite of the china I've seen. She smiled funny, and I knew she'd give it to me for Christmas.

She gave it to me for Christmas, 10 settings. Dinner plates, salad plates, bread plates, teacups, and saucers. Plus 10 little bowls I don't even know how to use. My mother didn't have those bowls.

I was so happy about my new china that I told my mother about it, but I didn't tell her about the bowls.

Well, she said, if I'd have known you wanted china, you could have had the set that's in the attic, the one from your grandfather. It was gray with little pink flowers and gold around the edges. He'd bought it piece by piece at gas stations as part of an ongoing promotion.

My mother didn't understand that I was excited about our matching china, couldn't understand that anyone would want to be like her. I don't understand why and spend a lot of time thinking about it.

I love my mother but sometimes I don't like her. I don't understand why. I spend a lot of time thinking about it.

WELCOME TO BOBCAT COUNTRY

We drove to the border just to say we pissed in the Mississippi
River, six in a car to see whether a Lifesaver makes a spark.
We danced in the headlights.

We had sex with boyfriends at the funeral home, slept with
the gym teacher. Snuck into the hot tub at the Holiday
Inn. Watched porn at Niemeyer's and went swimming and
swimming and swimming, held each other underwater too
long.

Our mothers chain-smoked, our fathers came straight home.
Everyone spoke the same language. Everyone felt the layoffs.

We taught gymnastics at the Y, sunned on rooftops, watched
MTV in the basement.

We rode our mopeds to Burger King, ate cheese curds at
Totem Bowl. We sucked on Atomic Fireballs, gobbled Runts
by the handful.

We waterskied at Okoboji in bikinis too big for our bodies.
Were thrown over shoulders, rode piggy-backed, played
chicken.

We waited outside the counselor's office trying to make the
phone ring. We moved in and out of lockers. We spit things.

We bought blue Wet-n-Wild nail polish, purple mascara,
wished for an extra quarter for Banana Yellow. We got our
ears double-pierced.

We detasseled corn for Agri-Pro, Pioneer. Worked ice cream
stands, gave friends free footlongs, sang Guns N' Roses songs.

We touched each other over our jeans. We celebrated six-month anniversaries, bought promise rings. We drove on the wrong side of the road with the lights out.

We went to every home football game, scooped the loop, peed in parking lots. We laughed hysterically and guessed who was having their period.

We didn't know for certain that others had lives that weren't like ours. We read *Sweet Valley High*.

We carved initials into our ankles, rode to funerals in pick-up trucks. We knew the deceased all our lives, whose dad beat who, whose sister got locked in the dog kennel.

Our mothers read Ann Landers and took naps in the afternoon, watched TV from a stool next to the kitchen counter.

We drove to Planned Parenthood, picked wedding colors. We listened to gangster rap in the stock room, ate at Perkins and Perkins and Perkins.

We drank in the barn, the backyard, the back room, the bedroom, the haunted house where they filmed *Twister*. We had the highest teen alcoholism rate in the state.

We let our hair bleach dry, took naps on towels, snapped pictures of our private parts. Talked on the phone for hours, ignored the flashing porchlights.

We shot each other with bottle rockets, drove T-top Trans Ams.

We ate salad bar with our grandmothers and dreamed in waterbeds with tiger-striped sheets.

We avoided the meat-packing plant, walked the train tracks. The only 22-year-old left in town bought us beer.

We promised we'd never tell. We believed everything we said.

Deer Wandered in From the Freeway

I.

Keep your antlers up and your mouth shut.
It's tough when you've lost your spots.
What gnaws you at night?
Vertical stripes, hospital corners—

orders you're so close to taking,
faking your way through rhododendron.
Are French doors the only way in?
Tricked like a deer in the breezeway,

a beveled tunnel of glass
passed as sanctuary until now.
How to pull through rough weather?
Together, strapped to the hood.

II.

All the women in my family
going about days dealing with age-
old forces beyond our control—
oppression, repression, depression—

we don't recognize and certainly
can't name, seeing just the line of light
on the windowpane of somewhere we know
we don't belong but when we kick it cuts,

blind fury, and only a few of us will scream
our way out, others kicking in the wrong places
and bleeding in the right ones, spending lifetimes
dying on the linoleum floor.

A History

When Tanya Anderson spent the night and told me, half
asleep, to use my finger and pretend like it was a boy, I did.

Watching a movie with my mom, Dolly Parton says "sax."
I asked Mom what it meant and she checked out a series of
books from the library. I knew what sex was, just not "sax."

I don't remember my first kiss.

I do remember Tony Kilbow, though, feeling me up for the
first time in Jackson Park after crawling through a pipe to an
empty storm drain. We couldn't look at each other, looked
instead at the Quiet Riot lyrics the high school kids painted
on the wall, stared at that rectangle of light like a mail slot to
the street. Listened to the cars.

I'd get up early to go running, sometimes sneaking through
the patio door and crawling into my boyfriend's bed in the
basement, five feet from his snoring brother. Everything still.
Hot after crunching through snow in blue lycra. The red
roar in my head.

We had sex on the laundry room floor, thin carpet over
cement.

In college, I'd get drunk and sleep with men I already cared
about as friends but then I'd cry. And sometimes they
weren't good friends.

My roommate, passing me in the kitchen said casually, "I
masturbate." I said, "Me too," although I didn't think I was
doing it right. She had shiny hair and straight teeth.

I had sex with the love of my life three times a day, almost flunked out of school. We went out to eat a lot.

Depression hit. What to do when you can't enjoy yourself? We didn't touch. Or talk.

Years passed.

Finally I realized he masturbated in the shower, no signs around the house. I had assumed because I wasn't, he wasn't either.

I'd turn away and cry.

Age 25? 26? It became cool to have sex-toy parties, like Tupperware, but this was too late.

Almost as late as my mother on the stairs, talking about sex for the first time since Dolly. I was seventeen.

Twenty-nine. The first by my hand alone. Twenty. Fucking. Nine.

For chrissake.

I guess I should be thankful I know even now.

ACROBATICS

I once went skinny-dipping in the dirtiest river in Europe,
and would again. I don't usually walk around naked,
even at home, but am good at swimming underwater,
can hold my breath for a long time. Sometimes at work
I make it to 56 seconds before wanting to pass out.
Sometimes passing out is nice. Did you know
that when an sea otter gives birth, she pulls the pup
from her while spinning circles, salty backflips?
I bet if I had to, I could do it too. I've been turning
somersaults my whole fucking life.

Me and You and Everyone We Know

When we ask for what we want and get it, we're terrified.

Do I look well to you guys? A lot of the time I wish I were the
younger sister and someone else had to go first. My sister
does that a lot, the nervous shaking, but stops when I hit
her. Same with cracking her knuckles.

I had a scrapbook like that, where I'd cut magazine pictures
out and organize them according to rooms in the house. I
miss knowing my neighbors, even if I didn't like them, or if
we didn't talk that much.

What have we done? We can't touch each other anymore, not
that we did anyway.

Christ I hate submitting poems. Art is a business like any
other and we take ourselves too seriously, everyone so weird
and desperate and alone. Is that the secret to everything?

The photos on the wall remind me of *Teen Beat*'s Ralph
Macchio, Corey Haim. Remember sliding beads on safety
pins? We hung them on our shoelaces, wore them on jean
jackets. I got a hope chest for my sixteenth birthday.

At a party once Tim Dwight lit Kristy's arm on fire.

I love how some couples instantly act like they're together.
I don't know how to be together and not together, which is
why I'm not good at dating. Austin and I look at each other
and brush our teeth, smiling, and it doesn't feel hokey. It just
feels like we can brush our teeth together.

We don't really want what we want. We want the wanting. *You think you deserve to feel that pain?*

Maybe I'll have kids so I can build tents out of sheets and furniture. *At least we are all together in this.* Is that what kids are, more to be in "together?"

Let's lie on our backs. I love it when people join others who are acting crazy, a kindness, like when Miranda helps hang the bird picture in the tree. I didn't even say a prayer for that bird I watched die at the airport.

THE THAW

There were only two African American
kids in my elementary school—
brother and sister. I remember their names
although many others have disappeared.
She wore tiny pink plastic bunny barrettes
like mine at the end of her braids.
He had a birthmark on his cheek darker
than the rest of his face. We all wore moon boots
and ran around in the snow, kicking it up,
melting it with heat from our skin,
our breath, until the dark earth beneath
pushed through, and we were tired of playing.

DOWN HOME

Nothing ever the matter, but something always. Mom in bed when we came home from school was normal.

In almost every childhood photo, Mom in the background, jaw set in a straight line, still and tense.

So angry. The only things she thought she could do for a living were to be a secretary, a stewardess, a teacher. Her hips too wide, they said, for the airplane aisle. No one told her things could be different and she never figured it out on her own.

She stayed in with the women while Dad went out—angry, maybe, that she had children. Angry he expected her to do everything and she never told him otherwise.

We walked around trying not to upset her, impossible. She was always already tired, seething.

RED WHITE AND BLUE

I wanted to be a cheerleader sitting along one edge of the
wrestling mat on red white and blue oversized square pillows
in a blue wrestling sweatshirt over a white turtleneck and
red white and blue polyester skirts with *rockets* or *bloomers*
or insert-term-for-underwear-you-wear-on-the-outside
underneath and a temporary tattoo of a cartoon bobcat
paw on my cheek my hair a ponytailed mass of spiral curls
sprayed stiff and shiny and mixed with red white and blue
ribbons in a tight, bouncy fit.

I wanted a varsity wrestler's last name screenprinted across
my ass and matching Kaepa shoes with the triangles that
pop out to swap between red white and blue colors plus
matching monogrammed socks to sit with my legs in a
swastika switching from left to right before putting my
hands back on my hips then pounding palms in unison—

RICK! IS! SU-PER FAN-TAS-TIC!
RICK! IS! SU-PER FAN-TAS-TIC!

—with jazz hands on the *tic* and anger in my fists without
knowing exactly why only it's fun to scream and growl and
groan cause I don't let myself do that at home I wanted
white teeth tan thighs the Roundhouse gymnasium dim
and spotlit bleachers up close and sweaty rust the wrestlers'
mothers I'd walk past carrying my red white and blue duffel
bag embroidered with my name and when I'd scream I'd say
everything I ever wanted to say.

RECURRING DREAM HOUSE

When you can move through a house blindfolded it belongs to you
—Michael Ondaatje

Mom moved across town years ago, took the oversized oak furniture. Its gloss clogs her shrunken living room, the dining table perpetually off balance.

Dad's left in honeycomb minus the bees, piles of phonebooks in corners. A Smurf poster and an oven mitt on top. The ancient microwave and everyone starting over and over.

This dream, the closet under the stairs. Dad's motorcycle helmet. For the first time, I wonder whether he wore it during the accident. A Mexican blanket, burgundy pants. An old guitar. A fire-proof safe.

Every car we've ever owned is in the driveway. My late-eighties Mustang a dull grey, Grandma's baby blue Nova. The two-tone Citation minus rusted floorboards. All the trunks are open.

Walking from one car to the next, my arms overflow with closet artifacts—jars of Grandpa's carrots, salmon in yellowing liquid, half-used cans of spray paint. However hard I look, every trunk is full.

I'm buried face-first in the foyer closet, shoulders weighted by the brush of musty fabrics. Dad's letter jacket's stiff, crinkling sleeves, striped cuffs. Mom's two giant down coats—one stained—with fake fur hoods. Dad's Army jacket, its weathered patches. His boy scout uniform, complete.

Layer after layer of brightly colored tulle sweeps my cheek, old ballet skirts. Ribbons and gold cloth. The prom dresses belonging to my sister and me, dirt coalescing in their folds. My red. Angie's purple. A sequin lands on my eyelash.

To get everything out, I pile on stocking caps, Grandpa's hunting vest, four-odd pairs of moonboots. Mismatched mittens. Stepping back to the linoleum, I'm dirty with cobwebs, Dusty's fur. I reach up to the dangling globe light, briefly touch its center. Watch it swing.

Dusty's nose smudges the window behind me, moist streaks as he jumps up and down. We always said he was the best looking one of the family. He refuses to let me pass, has yet to acknowledge any of us have left.

After the house was built, everything was chocolate. Sides the color of bark—rather, cracks in bark, a deeper shade. Off-white trim.

My nose in the dark carpet, I imagined dust mites—tiny pinchers—then smoothed my hair flat with a palm. Silky, I draped it over a stair, looked down.

The foyer already so far away.

The new occupants are here—a woman and her black-haired daughter. The girl is pissed, my stuff in her room, no space for her shoes. My bed pushed up under her window so she can crawl out too. The ballet poster in the yellow frame, my friends' autographs on the wall. She tosses her hair as I trace them.

My mother's old dresser stacked with shoeboxes, its roomy drawers and the tall mirror I reach through for objects—my father's vest and tie. My sister's porcelain bell collection. A black and pink skirt. Piecemeal satin swimming ribbons. A cedar box from the Ozarks.

The woman is home and I'm up to my knees in diaries. She pretends to understand. The girl's eyes flash brown velvet.

I sewed beads on those jeans, puff-painted others. That's my orange and green tie-dyed t-shirt from camp. Things cannot be left.

The daughter's fed up. I throw afghan on stuffed rabbit on hoop earrings on silver box on prom photo on souvenir button on baseball hat on sea glass on sewing kit on school ID. Leaning away from the mirror, I still can't see me.

The owners are coming home soon. A boy and his little brother are helping my sister and I gather our things. We look around the garage.

Where to start? The black metal boxes of mismatched nails? The garbage pails? Four bicycles hang from the ceiling.

We take inventory of what's on the shelves—one basketball, one bike pump (broken), a red and white Coleman cooler. Tennis balls, soil-crusted spade, holey gloves. Pogoball. Scuffed hula hoop, roller skates. A baton with turquoise glitter streamers.

The older brother winds the hose. The little one digs around for a booger, watching.

Ange steps around the grill, puts her hand on the hood of our third car. She pushes me around on the snowblower, lifts both boys in the wheelbarrow. Somebody's started the sprinkler.

There are many bedrooms here. One with garage sale
furniture shellacked pink and white. A desk, a bookcase. The
upper bunk that came crashing down when punched upward
with both feet, bedspread and matching sheets. Ruffles.

My parents' room. The brown duck that split in half to reveal
Dad's few trinkets—his gold and blue class ring, Army pins. A
wrinkled boutonniere, half-eaten roll of Certs. Mom's jewelry
box with identical strands of clunky beads—pink and red.
The black and white TV among sweaters in the closet to be
watched from bed, glasses of milk or iced tea on nightstands.
Paperback novels and self-help books spilling everywhere.

In my basement bedroom, I worried about burglars stepping
on me on their way in, rapists. Glow-in-the-dark stickers
stuck to the black beams of the unfinished ceiling, I'd listen
to the all-request dedication hour. *This one goes out from Stacy
to Phil on their six-month anniversary*—the glow of radio. I'd
spell the names of boys I had crushes on in the stars.

Ange's room in junior high never did feel like her, the
lavender, fifties-rock-and-roll theme I always hated.

Dad's den when he moved into it, his dresser and brown
duck. His black boxy briefcase with a Certs roll in the pocket.
The rowing machine. The twin bed.

I'm so mad Mom's not here to help pack the kitchen. I scream and scream but she won't hear. I scream into a koala bear-shaped cookie jar, a butterfly canister. Put my ear to the bundt cake pan. Lick the smooth oval divots of the Tupperware deviled egg carrier. I can't find a potholder.

There may have been a plant in the window above the sink, a heart-shaped sun catcher. There was something pale yellow and crocheted, sun filtering in.

Dad slammed the dishwasher, yelled, "I AM MAD!" I burst into tears, left the wet sponge on the counter, Sunday paper curling on the table.

Ange isn't here to help either and half of this goddamn bathroom used to be hers, her curlers green plastic spores around their spools. The cord around the box like a spiral white ribbon.

Her barrettes are in my drawer—the pink plastic rabbit ones, the blue lambs—but my hairbrush and eyeliner are in hers. Let's call it even.

The toilet brush and the Scrubbing Bubbles under the sink, so disappointed they didn't look like the ones in the commercial.

I put an old Easter basket full of headbands and drying nail polish into the clothes hamper in front of the toilet for safekeeping. Throw the *Reader's Digest* in there too. I don't know what I'm going to do about that giant mirror.

Dad sits on the porch swing, rocking back and forth with hairy, muscular calves. He's wearing jersey shorts and drinking unsweetened tea from his Coors mug. The sun starts to set as he gestures at the neighbor's yard.

Ange sits down next to him, barefoot and wishing she had a cigarette. She puts her head on his shoulder. He smiles his one-eyed smile.

I sit at the picnic table facing them, look through the sliding glass door to Mom doing dishes. I have a boyfriend to call but watch, feel my bangs brush my eyes, the ponytail down my back. My right foot tucked under my thigh.

Mom joins us, brings a piece of her chocolate cake in a white bowl. She carries a fork in the same hand, licks the fingers of the other.

The first star is out, a firefly blinks on nearby. It is warm. We are happy.

Epilogue

Ange is pregnant. She's bought diapers and something blue plastic "for baby." Of course, she didn't tell me, but lets me assume. I push someone aside to hug her.

I call in sick to work, call Mom and tell her to come immediately, leave Dad a voice mail.

Ange and I order pizza, the table wobbling even now. The whole house is hot.

Ange goes to turn on the front porch light. We have no front porch, but the wall connected to the garage is warm. Ange calls for me to look.

I don't believe her but come anyway, open the side door to the garage. Inside it's a clean burn, no flames. Like alcohol vapors or glimmers in the desert.

A golden retriever we never had squeezes past my leg, needs to go to the fenced-in patch of backyard. Flames begin to ripple from grey to blue to orange behind him in a backdraft, a sudden air suck, and he's on fire. I call and call but he won't come and I can't go to him, enveloped in gasoline fumes. I shut the door and leave him to burn.

Ange is already upstairs and out our old bedroom window. The room is empty with robin's egg blue carpet. I holler to make sure she's out and jump.

Across the street, we lean against the neighbor's house, squat down. Together, we look back and wait for firemen who aren't coming.

DRUGSTORE COWGIRL

Just leave me alone with the girl in the casserole
—Tina Brown Celona

PHILOSOPHY FOR THE PERIPATETIC

It's 3:35 on Sunday, December fourth. Paper bag at my feet,
an Asian woman by the El doors asleep in a graceful curve.
A man with a lawn chair and foil-wrapped plate, a redhead
with Christmas-ribbon curls looks kind. I am aching,
out of my mind. In my chest, a bicycle bell clangs, sound
waves slipping out like mercury through fish. I want to desist,
resist this edacity like birch skin, paper thin, quite
a sheen. I want all bad glow to go, to leave just the tree's
heart in the middle of middles. I want to be only good.

MATERNITY

Cab drivers need to stop telling me to have babies.
Coming home from a party, I told one I just turned
thirty. He asked, *Don't you deserve to have someone
call you Mommy?* I didn't know. Later, a cabbie talked
about his daughters, showed me pictures of grandkids.
He told me he loved me, said my parents missed me,
and asked about my job—*No cab driving for you,*
he said, *no cabs for you. You'd be a good mother,
I can tell,* he said. *I love you like a daughter
and I can tell,* he said, *I love you.*
I would *be a good mother,* I said, and told him
I loved him back.

Dear Evil

Landlady, when you fixed my roof,
it leaked two weeks later. January was warm
this year. I don't care what you say, I only had one
"beer party." It was the goddamn Fourth of July. No,
you can't have my goldfish tumblers. No, you cannot
buy them. When I was mugged outside the building,
you charged me to change the locks.

WHEN I GROW UP I WANT TO BE NATALIE DEE

If I were Natalie Dee, I might not
have back fat. Then again, I might.

If I were Natalie Dee, I could think
about hot dogs, diet soda, and small
furry animals all day long.
And snakes.

I could draw pictures of myself
with fists full of tampons in the air.

If I were Natalie Dee, and she was me,
I would have a boyfriend, and smoke,
and my boyfriend and I would smoke
together. Hamburgers would have wings.
Cupcakes would have fangs.

If I were Natalie Dee, I would think
things like, "It is Bucket Day
everyday!" and "Cactus: Not much better
than no cactus." I could have a penis
or go into space any time I wanted.

My boyfriend and I would play games
like "What's in My Pants?" or "Don't
Call Me Larry, Larry!" and one of my eyes
would squint more than the other.
Actually, it does.

For Poets (& Others)

At readings, two drinks, minimum, will make you as
brilliant as you think you are. This goes for the audience too.

Never write poems using the following words, mainly
because it will annoy me: blackberries, poppies, detritus,
bifurcation, sluiced, slaked.

James Wright has already seen horses in a field.

Do not admit to being a poet unless asked directly. It's like
saying your grandmother died. Maybe you weren't close with
your grandmother? People don't know what to do.

Get a bad haircut and pretend it's a good one.

Get used to disappointing your mother.

Write poems with these words in them: Squirrel. Rabbit.
Rabbits are the new monkeys, they're just funny.

Learn to read aloud without "poet voice"—that long,
overdrawn singsong. Are you *trying* to put your audience to
sleep?

Respect. Earn it. Use it. Own it. Being nice gets you a lot
further than being a dick.

Develop at least one addiction.

When asked whether you've experimented with the opposite
sex, say yes. Otherwise, people don't know what to do.

Memorize at least one of your own poems to perform on command. It's an engagement story you'll be asked to repeat for the rest of your life.

Do not list your Pushcart Prize nomination in your bio. I mean, ever.

Be hot. Things will go easier for you and you'll get plenty of action.

OR, be good. Be very, very good and you'll get plenty of action.

Thank your parents. They put you here, even if you don't like it. Not liking it makes for some good poetry.

Do not have birds on your book cover, mainly because it will annoy me.

Use your real name because you are not a rock star. If you want to be a rock star, learn to play an instrument.

Brush your teeth. Nobody likes a poet with four teeth.

Never, ever write poems about being a poet. Publishers don't like them. Instead, substitute every instance of the word "poet" with "rabbit."

Then send the poem to me.

MY MOTHER CAN'T STAND THIS POEM

Like how my sister hates the word "crotch,"
which I say to piss her off. But I also admit
I like it—the word with its long *ahhhh* sound.
Crahhhhhtch, as in when I want my sister to
hold my drink in the car, I say "Can you crotch this
for a second?" Sometimes when I hate a girl,
I say she needs a good "crotch-kicking."
There's crotch rockets, fire crotches, always
crotch rot—and in magazines, paparazzi,
all those crotch-sh*aahhhh*ts.

Taxonomy Lessons

They're jealous of you they just don't know it yet, said Sarah
to me once over merlot at Gioco. I think of this often, like
when Kristen announces she's getting married, making me the
last of our group not to be.

I think of this when the first dress goes over Kristen's head,
and she looks so beautiful I pause. Discussing details, her
groom-to-be turns a little green and she pats his hand smiling.

Sarah tells me anyone can be married, have children, own
a house. Why be just anyone she says, when you can be
someone?

Sarah goes on to say that I'm a peacock while others are
pigeons. Not that there's anything wrong with being a
pigeon she says, pigeons are honorable creatures. You're just a
peacock. Why do you want to be a pigeon!

I can think of plenty of reasons I say. What will my mother
tell her friends? Small talk stops when people find out what I
am. Pigeons are puzzled by peacocks.

Let them be puzzled she says. You are a beautiful Indian Blue!

But I've lived my whole life among pigeons I say. I don't know
how to be a peacock. I'm scared of peacocks. I am a pigeon!

Jennifer tries to solve the problem. You are neither peacock
nor pigeon she says, but a combination. Something like a
jackalope she says, not one or the other.

What "one" or "the other" was, Jennifer didn't say.

Still, the pigeons and I know something's not right. Am I then a robin among sparrows? Close to passing, with this bright red burning I keep trying to hide.

Drugstore Cowgirl

Do they really put shards of fiberglass in lip balm?
Pastiche, pastiche. Collage away.
I am not a poem-writer. I am a poem-MAKER! Cut
and paste. Where are the strings? Blow me a kiss,
Babe, let's go to Walgreen's. I'm out of mascara,
need to make me some masks. My eyes. My eyes!
Oh, the man in the ushanka. They gave me
too much change!

Why I Hate Ian Harris

When I meet a poet who is jealous of the poems of others . . .
I'm sure that poet has not yet written a poem as good as he
knows he can. —Richard Hugo

He makes me think Hugo was right,
every week pulling brilliant poems from his ass
about art or love or banana boats
but never really doing the assignment.
I've heard he's a doctor's kid though,
which I think about when I burn my forehead
with the curling iron or pinch my fingers
in the door because I'm distracted
and tired, always tired, and thinking money
begets money and maybe his college
was paid for so maybe he spends days
on his poems. My Dad and I, however,
got three loans that can't be combined,
so I have three payments
for a degree my Dad said would,
with a quarter, buy me a cup of coffee.
He meant it in a good way really,
trying to point out my general lack
of responsibility or rationality or anything
that might help me take care of myself.
Besides, I had a dream last night
that my Dad gave me poems.
I dreamt my class was camping somewhere
that looked suspiciously like a trailer park
and on my bunk my Dad left framed poems
hooked together with chicken wire
like Christmas lights or something from Ikea.
My Dad who wouldn't read poetry if it killed him.
And he had known all my favorites,

had LaserJet printed them in color, and on waking
I knew I'm really not that tired,
I love my father,
and Ian Harris is just fucking good.

IOWA POETS

Attending the Writer's Workshop
does not make you an Iowa poet.
You never drove Highway 30 to Vet's
Auditorium for the Tourney—a line
of Camaros full of Busch Light and Cloves,
turquoise Geo Trackers with shoe-polished
windows. You never detasseled corn
or worked as a checker at Hy-Vee
until college, returning summers
to get schnockered playing Three Man
in someone's basement. Never showed
sheep at the state fair, saw the butter
sculptures like Tibetan monks. No
four-wheelers or grill-your-own-steak
restaurants. So, go ahead.
Write your poems about fields
and farmers and quiet, how
you can see the stars every night.
You'll never love them like I do.

Semantics

I used to be able to jump up, touch my toes, and land
on my back, to turn four times without stopping.
Now I want to spin forever. Infinity symbol,
a perfect circle. Contributing and contributed to,
the motion of stars, perpetually new constellations.
A station where trains arrive and depart, vasculature.
Hula hoop steady at the hips, a jump rope
without a miss. A clear and constant stream—
the medium not the middle.

MOBILE HOMECOMING

Anyway, poor everyone who never went to Harvard
—Chelsey Minnis

PASSING A FEDERAL BUILDING, MY MOTHER ASKS WHETHER THERE'LL BE A PARADE

Because we're walking next to barricades.
I tell her no, they're to prevent drive-up
truck bombings like Oklahoma City.

Later she packs my sister and me crates
of canned food and bottled water,
toilet paper, flashlights, a hand-

powered radio. Just in case, she says.
When I tell her I might move to Oklahoma,
she turns away, talks about tornadoes.

MOBILE HOMECOMING

My professor said I was "aiming for mediocrity." I was thirty years old. My mother's into money recently, talks about some book that associates class with worldviews of material goods. In the book, low class means "quantity," middle class means "quality," and high class means "presentation." Working on my master's degree, I knew for certain I wasn't middle class, going again for quantity. I saw that others, hello Professor, viewed me as *not* middle class. That I was low-middle class, or low-class, even, depending on how much cash the one doing the viewing had. Or really that I was culturally bankrupt from growing up in a vacuum cleaner.

I grew up in a nice house on the good side of town with parents who loved me and a shotgun rack in the basement. For vacation money, my mother worked part-time at Wal-Mart. My friends and I wore Daisy Dukes and steel-toe boots, drank Zima through licorice straws. Punched out dome lights, plundered construction sites. The boys we loved wore Carhartt coats and Coed Naked t-shirts. We rode in cars chased out of town, were raised on mayonnaise. What can I say—my professor was right. Someone's looking down on my kinds of comfort. I grew up in a nice house on the good side of town with parents who once owned a mobile home. My father shot a rattlesnake in the driveway. He stopped it before it got to the dogs.

Tobacco as a Remedy for Suicide

Dickens thought smoking a pipe could prevent suicide. Kurt Vonnegut just died. In 1984, he tried to kill himself. His mother killed herself.

Vonnegut, however, knew smoking was a "fairly honorable form of suicide" so he smoked unfiltered Pall Malls. I don't know what Grandmother smoked but she had a nervous breakdown when Mom was born.

I had a nervous breakdown two weeks ago. Weltschmerz probably. German has all the good words.

"Vonnegut" is German. He once said "I am a monopolar depressive descended from monopolar depressives. That's how come I write so good."

I write pretty good too I guess. Aunt Jackie writes me letters. Mom won't talk about the breakdown so maybe I'll ask Jackie what happened. Grandmother may have tried to kill herself, and I deserve to know.

ARE YOU GONNA WAKE UP

On the way to work this morning, a tall blond man locked
his blue eyes with mine and asked, loudly, *Are you gonna
wake up tomorrow young-er, with all the money you've made?*
Boy was I angry.

I was angry all the way to work. He must've thought I live in
one of the four new condo buildings on the block, but I live
in a tiny two-bedroom with slanted floors and a roof that
leaks in four places. My bathroom's so small you can sit on
the toilet and throw up in the sink simultaneously. Not that
I've done this. I'm just saying.

What did he know, I thought. By this time I was at work,
a pharmaceutical advertising agency. Boy was I angry.
Pharmaceutical companies have to make money somehow.
Their drugs keep me from spending days locked in my office
crying like I used to. I'm just saying. They keep me from
having babies.

Because I don't want babies right now I'm one of five blonde
women without power in a boardroom. We're listening to
three men with power discuss endometrial ablation. Sketches
of a uterus made of water. Of uterus as shield. As bull, as lily.
The Great Wall.

The Hoover Dam.

Because I don't want to be locked in my office crying like I
used to I receive daily updates called "Vaginitis Hotsheets."
It's not like I dreamt of doing this, but I used to spend
money to make myself happy so I didn't have any. Because I
didn't have any I needed to make myself happy.

How many of us end up where we actually want to go? A bathroom where you can sit on the toilet and throw up simultaneously. It's not like I dreamt of doing this. Are we gonna wake up tomorrow young-er, with all the money we've made? I'm just saying. What does he know.

Reality TV Has Ruined My Childhood

I.

Kate's mom redecorated Kate's entire childhood home by
theme, featuring Greek, African, and Egyptian rooms. Ionic
columns next to the bath and a giraffe in the basement.

The problem, however, is that Kate's mom mixes artifacts—
pyramid plant stand next to Aphrodite—and throws in what
she likes. *American Gothic* next to Tutankhamen, a loon and
a Nuna mask on a shelf.

Kate says her mom's been watching "Trading Spaces," and
I know this is happening across the Midwest, farmhouses
being furnished one Cost Plus World Market piece at a time.

II.

My mom, bless her, has a purple wall. She tells me what her friends say and I picture her trying to ignore them. Why just one wall? They say. And purple, too!

Mom, I say, it's perfectly fine to paint just one wall. In fact, Kate has a purple wall just like that.

She does? Mom says.

Yes, I say, just one.

MOTHER AND SISTER MINUS THE BODY

I have not held them
nearly enough—
suddenly desperate
for it, ear to shoulder
over the long
drive home.

GAMES WE PLAY

Once when we were little and had sleepovers we invented
a game. One girl was locked out of the room and the rest
of us rated her, on a scale of 1 to 10, as a friend. Most of us
averaged around 7, 7.5.

When we were older, we spent a lot of time thinking about
how cruel we were as kids, how we kicked our friends out
of the room and judged them on a scale of 1 to 10. Kids are
just cruel we'd think, shaking our heads.

Not long ago, working in Corporate America, we filled out
a series of forms. Each form was a performance evaluation
for each coworker. This is what's known as a "360-degree
review." We weren't that cruel after all we thought.

Working in Corporate America, we distract ourselves by
watching television shows. We like the ones where the
characters are just like us, or the "us" we'd like to be. We
spend a lot of time thinking about which *Sex in the City*
character we are, deciding whether we should buy "I'm a
Miranda" t-shirts. Except no one really wants to be her, and
we don't know any Samanthas.

We used to distract ourselves by watching *Friends*. Which
of us is a Rachel? A Monica? None of us could be Phoebe
'cause she used to live on the streets like the people in back
of our building. All of us wanted to sleep with Joey, really,
though we said Ross.

When we were little and had sleepovers distracting ourselves
used to be much easier. Someone wanted to be Ariel in
Footloose, those red boots, or the blonde girl who drove the
car. Even then, we could always find a Sarah Jessica Parker.

Sarah Jessica, man. She just seemed so nice. We'd give her a 9. An 8.5 for sure.

Two Nights With The Composer

I.

The first time it happened we were eating dinner with my sister. The Composer was spacey and distant and I thought it was because my sister doesn't talk, so I was going on about my day, joking and ignoring things.

We made it to the cinemaplex before The Composer got woozy on the escalator. I was holding him up by his collar and a security guard asked if we were all right, held the elevator, watched me help The Composer into a cab.

They handcuffed The Composer to the hospital bed. A nurse brought a tube of black goo he was supposed to drink. He didn't like the black goo, kept spitting it out and crying. I was begging him to drink it. I wasn't crying.

Suicide attempts have security in their rooms. A guard stood in the corner for over an hour, looking embarrassed and watching me beg The Composer to drink the black goo. The Composer kept spitting it out and crying.

II.

The second time it happened, The Composer was home
alone but called his mother in South Carolina who called the
cops who broke into his apartment to get him. I was sitting
by The Composer's hospital bed when the ex-girlfriend-The-
Composer-left-for-me showed up.

She sat on one side of the bed, me on the other. We were
shaky and pale. Nobody said anything. The ex-girlfriend-
The-Composer-left-for-me held one of his hands. I held the
other.

When the ex-girlfriend was gone, an orderly came in and
said there was a bet on who would last longer. Apparently I
had won him some money. He said it was me all the way.

MATURITY

Recently I realized I am a grown-up. Hrm, I thought.
But that's not a very interesting thing for a grown-up
to think. I mean, I've known all along but I didn't really
know. Suddenly it was as if my body had slipped
through a prison cell, a window, the front gate. The bars
were close. When I emerged on the other side,
my whole element popped loose. *Boinggggg!*
The squishing didn't matter, just the bursting,
Athena-style, fully formed. I stood, reverberating.
I had done the thing I'd been waiting
my whole (now immaterial) life to do.

BEDSIDE MANNERS

I met MaryAnne at the hospital, so distracted I could hardly
see straight. She was making small talk and trying to be cool
but I was fine. I was perfectly fine until she left and you
arrived, Dr. Marcus, with your pasty anesthesiologist face.

Why am I here? you asked. I didn't know. *It's unusual that
I'd be here*, you said. *Can you tell me why I'm here?* I didn't
understand. You were looking at my chart, Dr. Marcus,
when you asked, *Well why are YOU here?*

I'm here because I'm depressed, I said, and started to cry. You
bastard. You put your arm around me and said you'd see me
in obstetrics soon. As if I wanted that. You were trying to be
cool, Dr. Marcus, said I looked like Gwyneth Paltrow.

After surgery I was fine. I was perfectly fine. When I could
walk, you said, *There she is! How are you feeling Gwyneth?*

I wanted you to die, Dr. Marcus. I hope you felt that when I
looked at you. So badly, Dr. Marcus, I couldn't see straight.

I Am Falling for You America

I don't visit my sister when she's recovering because it reminds me that she's been depressed for a long time. I just can't watch a movie with her, eating takeout and pretending it's fun, when I have a hundred things to do because I'm trying to make something of myself.

I have to think my family needs me to make something of myself. This way, I can sit outside the Laundromat at 9:30 in early fall, writing and eating a Blue Bunny ice cream cookie, and call it work. This way I do not have to visit my sister, can wash the laundry a month overdue.

On the way here, there was a stencil on the sidewalk with "I am falling for you" below it. I'd seen it before and thought, oh how cute, sometimes I love the city. Most of the time I don't. Cities are where people who are trying to make something of themselves end up, drinking bottled water and sitting outside the Laundromat.

Above "I am falling for you," the picture was of two smiley-faced buildings holding hands. How cute, I thought, I love this city. But then one had a plane flying into it and the other had smoke coming out of it. Is this sick or wonderful? America, I am falling for you.

Last week a pitcher drove his plane into a Manhattan building. I'm so tired of being afraid all the time. As if that's a problem for a middle-class white girl trying to live a collective dream of being Brad Pitt, or married to him. I am terrified less than most.

When Diane Sawyer interviewed Brad Pitt, the network showed footage of his trip to Africa. How strange that starving Ethiopians knew Brad Pitt, but they did, had pooled the day's bread to make one large piece like a giant cookie from the mall. Their eyes were wide and they were clapping. Brad Pitt, I am falling for you.

My ice cream cookie is gone. I'm outside the Laundromat writing and calling it work because now my fingers are cold. I'm tired of trying to become somebody. Once, waiting in a doorway with MaryAnne, I was hungover and wanted to eat too much, a pizza, a giant cookie. Then she said I mean, what did we go to war for? And looked at me.

To free the Iraqi people I said, and the look on her face reminded me it wasn't true. I knew it wasn't true too. I saw smoke from one building and a plane flying into another and was tired of being afraid all the time, as only a middle-class white girl trying to become somebody can be. I am falling for you, America. America, I am falling.

ALL THE WAY AROUND THE DIAL

Today I realized The Hold Steady was singing about John Berryman, and damn if they weren't describing my past and present selves in the place those along the actual border refer to as *Illowa*. Driving to Iowa for Thanksgiving, Skid Row plays on the radio and my sister and I sing and think about Sebastian Bach throwing a bottle at fans.

We're on our way back to Cedar Rapids because Mom doesn't live in Marshalltown anymore and Dad moved to Vegas with a new wife, which sounds worse than it is. Besides, Chicago is home now the only way a city of three million can be home to one person, like Vonnegut thinking it ridiculous to be a U.S. citizen. But I have started to miss the noise when I leave.

After the tolls, I seek out the bare hill with the perpetually burning flame as if the Olympic Torch lived in DuPage county. It's violet and orange and probably refuse, beautiful and violent. I look for it anyway.

We drive through Dixon, Reagan's hometown, and get nostalgic for Max Headroom, Coca-Cola, our father. We drive past the first Wal-Mart in months, stop at Arby's where a blind employee is singing 'Jolene' by a pink plastic Christmas tree with no lights.

See how the people are already different? Thicker? A teenager in a BV letter jacket reminds me of my "bacterial vaginosis" account at work, but I don't tell my sister, enjoy my funny secret.

Later, we pass Atkinson Road and the theme of our junior-high lock-in—Tesla's 'Love Song'—comes on. Damn if I don't still know all the words. Lights are flickering through the graying fields and I wish they were bonfires, stare hard trying to tell.

Here's where it happens, by the border. All the way around the dial with no anchor. I've felt like this before, walking to an empty seat on the train, brushing past the preacher on State Street, or stumbling across a bumper—I mean, a whole fender—in the middle of the sidewalk. Everything falling away, the dial spinning, and for a moment I know we are truly alone. Nobody watching, no hands outstretched save our own.

My eyes glaze over and I am moving but no longer inside.

Something catches, 100.3 WLIV Luv FM maybe, and I recognize the shoes on the metal grate—on the dash—as mine. We pass a combine aglow like a firefly. I'm writing this by the dome light. My sister no longer minds, is picturing Mom coming to the bowling alley to pick her up and take her home.

NOTES

For Poets (& Others)

The title rips off the title of Shanna Compton's book *For Girls (& Others)*.

Me and You and Everyone We Know

The title is taken from the film of the same name by Miranda July.

Recurring Dream House

This section was composed entirely during a residency at the Ragdale Foundation.

Tobacco as a Remedy for Suicide

The title is an opinion attributed to Charles Dickens in the notes from Van Gogh's letters, Penguin edition.

When I Grow Up I Want to Be Natalie Dee

Thanks to Natalie Dee, Jamesy G., and Davey A. Visit www.nataliedee.com.

Why I Hate Ian Harris

Many, many thanks to Ian.

ACKNOWLEDGEMENTS

Many thanks to the editors of the following publications, in which some of these poems first appeared: *Anti-, Arsenic Lobster, blossombones, Buffalo Carp, Coe Review, Columbia Poetry Review, Denver Quarterly, Elephant, Foursquare, MiPOesias, MoonLit, Sawbuck,* and *Wicked Alice.*

Sincere thanks to the following for their ever-important support, in its varying forms: Addie Palin, Becca Klaver, Beth Ann Fennelly, Chad Heltzel, Clay Matthews, Columbia College Chicago, Garrett Brown, Hanna Andrews, Jennifer L. Knox, Melissa Severin, Michael Robins, the Ragdale Foundation, Selah Saterstrom, Shearsman Books, Steven D. Schroeder, Tony Frazer, and the Women of Switchback Books—past, present, and future.

Unwavering thanks to (and for!) the ladies: Maryann Homan, Erin Ingle, Aunt Jackie, Aunt Dixie, Aunt Gerry, Kristy Stewart, Kristen Chamberlain, Beth Meier, Jessi Lee Gaylord, MaryAnne Lyons, Mary Biddinger, Simone Muench, Kristy Bowen, Cathy Nieciecki, Daniela Olszewska, Erika Snell, Amy Blevins, Julie Gerut, and Jana Ireijo.

Finally, thanks to Mom, Dad, and Ange for being brave.
I love you.